Emily Dickinson

Self-Discipline in the Service of Art

Emily Dickinson
Self-Discipline in the Service of Art

Carl Rollyson
&
Lisa Paddock

ASJA Press
New York Bloomington

Emily Dickinson:
Self-Discipline in the Service of Art

Copyright © 2009 by Carl Rollyson

*All rights reserved. No part of this book may be used
or reproduced by any means, graphic, electronic, or
mechanical, including photocopying, recording, taping or
by any information storage retrieval system without the
written permission of the publisher except in the case of brief
quotations embodied in critical articles and reviews.
The views expressed in this work are solely those of the author
and do not necessarily reflect the views of the publisher, and
the publisher hereby disclaims any responsibility for them.*

*ASJA Press
An imprint of iUniverse, Inc*

iUniverse books may be ordered through booksellers or by contacting:

*iUniverse
1663 Liberty Drive
Bloomington, IN 47403
www.iuniverse.com
1-800-Authors (1-800-288-4677)*

*Because of the dynamic nature of the Internet, any Web addresses or
links contained in this book may have changed since publication and
may no longer be valid. The views expressed in this work are solely those
of the author and do not necessarily reflect the views of the publisher,
and the publisher hereby disclaims any responsibility for them.*

ISBN: 978-1-4401-1534-9 (sc)

Printed in the United States of America

iUniverse rev. date:01/08/08

Table of Contents

TIMELINE i

PROLOGUE: Self-Discipline v

CHAPTER 1: "The Birds That Stay" 1

CHAPTER 2: Now and Forever 6

CHAPTER 3: To Be Great--"Like Mr. Michael Angelo" 10

CHPTER 4: Love and War and Famine 15

CHPTER 5: The Aftermath 20

CHAPTER 6: Revival and Loss 24

CHAPTER 7: "Home is so far from Home" 29

CHAPTER 8: "The Mind Alone without Corporeal Friend" .. 35

SUMMING UP A LIFE 39

AFTERWORD TO PARENTS 41

BIBLIOGRAPHY 43

GLOSSARY 47

TIMELINE

1830:
December 10: Emily Dickinson is born in Amherst, Massachusetts.

1844:
The Republic of Texas is annexed by the United States.

1846:
June 15: The United States divides the Oregon Country with Great Britain. The area below the 49th parallel becomes U.S. territory, while that above joins the Dominion of Canada.
May 13: The United States declares war on Mexico after eleven Americans are killed in a border dispute.

1848:
January 24: Gold is discovered at Sutter's Creek, setting off the California Gold Rush.
February 2: The Treaty of Guadalupe Hidalgo ends the Mexican-American War.
July 19: A group meeting in Seneca Falls, New York, demands equal rights for women, such as the right to vote.

Emily Dickinson completes her formal schooling.

1856:
July: Austin Dickinson, Emily's brother, marries Susan Gilbert.

1857:

March 6: The United States Supreme Court declares that slaves are not citizens.

1858:

Emily Dickinson writes her first poems.

1861:

April 12: The Civil War formally begins when Confederate soldiers fire on Union troops in Ft. Sumter, South Carolina.

1862:

The peak year of Emily's productivity as a poet, the year she falls in love--probably with Pastor Charles Wadsworth--and begins writing to the essayist and social reformer Thomas Wentworth Higginson.

1865:

April 9: The Civil War ends when Confederate General Robert E. Lee surrenders at Appomattox Courthouse, Virginia, to the commander of the Union forces, General Ulysses S. Grant.

April 14: President Abraham Lincoln is assassinated by the actor and Confederate supporter John Wilkes Booth while attending a play at Ford's Theater in Washington, D.C.

1866:

"A narrow fellow in the grass," one of only a handful of Emily's poems published during her lifetime, appears against her wishes in *The Springfield Republican*.

1870:
Emily turns forty and Colonel Higginson visits Emily for the first time.

1874:
June 16: Emily's father, Edward Dickinson, dies.

1875:
Emily establishes a friendship with fellow poet Helen Hunt Jackson.

1877:
Emily is courted by family friends Samuel Bowles and Otis Lord.

1881:
July 2: President James A. Garfield is assassinated in a Washington, D.C. train station by a mentally ill man with no clear motive.

Mabel Loomis Todd, the wife of an astronomy professor at the local college, arrives in Amherst and befriends Emily.

1882:
November: Emily's mother--also named Emily--dies.

1883:
October: Emily's eight-year-old nephew, Gilbert, dies.

1884:
March: Judge Lord dies
June: Emily suffers a nervous breakdown.

1885:
August: Helen Hunt Jackson unexpectedly dies.

1888:
May 15: Emily Dickinson dies of Bright's Disease in Amherst, Massachusetts.

PROLOGUE
Self-Discipline

Self-discipline involves training and controlling yourself--particularly your passions, your desires, and above all your conduct. Often, we associate self-discipline with personal improvement, such as losing weight or training for a sport. But self-discipline is an essential virtue for anyone who wants to govern his or her own personality and conduct. Without self-discipline, it is difficult--if not impossible--to maintain a steady record of achievement and success. Yet, truly self-disciplined people are less interested in whether the world applauds their achievements than in their own sense of personal accomplishment.

By any measure, the 19th-century American poet Emily Dickinson exemplified the virtue of self-discipline. She wrote poetry largely for her own pleasure and to exercise and increase her creative talents. Very few of her poems were published during her own lifetime, yet we know that she wrote consistently--perhaps every day--over several decades. Poetry was her way of knowing herself and understanding the world. She could control and express her ideas and emotions through poetry, perhaps the most demanding form of writing.

What does it mean to be a disciplined poet? It means writing and rewriting poems until they seem to be as perfect as possible. Dickinson left behind many drafts of her poems--sometimes including alternate wordings, as if to acknowledge that her writing was still seeking perfection.

Dickinson's discipline was self-imposed. She met no publishing deadlines. She did not write for a patron who sponsored her creative efforts. She did not expect the world to acknowledge her poetry as soon as it was written. Yet now she is considered one of the greatest poets ever to have written in the English language. She valued the labor and the results of a job well done. Emily Dickinson is a model not only for writers, but for anyone who wishes calmly and determinedly to pursue a goal, even without the prospect of an immediate reward..

Dickinson's quiet life at home also shows us how a person can lead a life that is rich and rewarding while not taking part in great events or even being known beyond a small circle of friends.

CHAPTER 1
"The Birds That Stay"

Emily Dickinson was born, lived, and died in the same house. Although she did visit Washington, D.C., Boston, and Philadelphia, she rarely traveled, spending most of her life in Amherst, Massachusetts, a college town that in the first half of the nineteenth century consisted of some 3,000 people. She was named after her mother, who was then a full participant in the life of Amherst, winning cooking contests and doing her part to aid the poor and perform other charitable services. The younger Emily had a narrow but stimulating circle of friends--many of them important writers and prominent citizens. She liked to stay at home. Home was her natural habitat, and she had no urge to migrate to other places. Neither did her older brother, Austin, or her younger sister, Lavinia, with whom Emily always lived. As Emily put it in one of her poems, "We are the birds that stay."

> *Emily Dickinson's retirement from the world had... a tradition behind it... it has always been a possible way of life for New England spinsters and widows....*
>
> --George Frisbie Whicher,
> Emily Dickinson biographer

Significantly, the home Emily was born in was called the Homestead. It was one of the grandest houses in town, an imposing brick structure that looks--and still looks--almost like a government building--the kind you might see in Philadelphia if you visited the Liberty Bell and the Independence Hall area.

The house and the atmosphere of the town could easily make Emily feel that she lived in an important place. Ideas and religious beliefs were taken seriously in Amherst. Emily's father, Edward Dickinson, was as imposing looking as his house. His approach to life was equally formidable. In his proposal to his wife he wrote: "My life must be a life of business, of labor and application to the study of my profession." Educated at Amherst College and Yale University, he became one of Amherst's most prominent lawyers as well as a member of the United States Congress.

> *The village of Amherst was famous for having more ministers per capita that any other town in the United States.*
>
> --Jay Leyda, a scholar of Dickinson's work

Emily respected her father, but relations between father and daughter were rather strained. Edward Dickinson may not have known what to do with his bright, imaginative daughter. There was little place in 19th-century America for independent-thinking women. Women were expected to marry and to raise a family. Those who did not became spinsters, single females usually supported by their families. A few women had careers, but they were definitely not to be found among the citizens of Amherst.

Of her father Emily observed: "He buys me many Books--but begs me not to read them--because he fears they joggle the mind." It is a revealing sentence. Edward realized that his daughter deserved an education, yet he held the notion, a common one for that time, that too much study might rattle a woman's brain, which was thought to be smaller than a man's.

No one knows for sure what Emily thought of her father's rather confused attitude towards her, but her comments suggest she kept some distance from him--as she did from most males who treated her as an inferior. She was not rebellious. But she did not fear exercising her mind or finding a way to her own beliefs. With words she could take the measure of anyone, and the precise use of words became a kind of daily discipline for her.

Emily's father's imagination could not stretch as far as her own. In a letter she observed: "Father says in fugitive moments when he forgets the barrister and lapses into the man, says that his life has been passed in a wilderness, or an island. . . ." In other words, when Edward Dickinson was not being a man of the world and accomplishing things, he lapsed (briefly) into a rather grim view of existence that isolated him from other people.

Emily may have shared some of her father's sense of isolation, but she had wit and an empathy for others that made her life anything but sad or lonely. She knew all about human society, and if she participated in it sparingly, she did so by choice.

Emily's father sent her to Amherst Academy, which was founded by her own grandfather, Samuel Fowler Dickinson, and Noah Webster, the author of one of the first American dictionaries. At Amherst Academy, Emily studied four subjects, which she called "Mental Philosophy, Geology, Latin, and Botany." She also went to Mount Holyoke Female Academy in South Hadley, Massachusetts, where she stayed for one year. For her time, she was well educated--particularly for a woman--and she did much studying beyond the basic subjects she took at school.

Emily thought of herself as pretty. At fourteen, she told a girlfriend, "I am growing handsome very fast indeed! I expect I shall be the belle of Amherst when I reach my 17rh year." The one existing photograph of her was in fact taken when she was 17 years old, but it conveys an impression of plainness. Both Emily and her brother objected that it did not do her justice. The photograph shows her to have an oval face, rather full lips, and dark, inquiring eyes. She once gave this flirtatious description of herself to a male correspondent: "I am small, like the Wren, and my Hair is bold, like the Chestnut Bur--and my eyes, like the Sherry in the Glass, that the Guest leaves."

Clearly, Emily felt closest to birds. Their quick movements and darting flight find their counterparts in her delicate but bold writing. As a bird that stays, she customarily reserved her high spirits for her poetry and for her friends. As one critic of her work says, she thought of poetry as the house she lived in. She felt safe, comfortable, and courageous when she was writing. Poetry is what rooted her in Amherst, and Amherst in turn grounded her poetry.

Points to ponder

- Emily Dickinson led a quiet life, but this did not mean that for her there were no adventures. What do you think makes life worth living for a stay-at-home poet?

- Emily Dickinson used the language of poetry to acquire self-discipline. What was it about using words precisely that helped her lead a fulfilling life?

CHAPTER 2
Now and Forever

Emily Dickinson thought that in many ways childhood was the freshest time of life, when you can see things with more intensity than adults do. Adults get caught up in routines, in their jobs, and in other responsibilities. Children just experience life in the moment. And it is the "nowness" of childhood that Emily missed most as she was growing up. In a random note she scribbled on the back of a newspaper clipping, she recollected a humorous moment when her youthful immersion in a momentary sensation ran up against her mother's sensibility:

"Two things I have lost with Childhood--the rapture of losing my shoe in the Mud and going Home barefoot." Mother was cross about the lost shoe, but she "frowned with a smile," because she, too, remembered the strong, joyous feelings she experienced in her early encounters with nature, when the world was new to her.

The world of childhood is immediate and pressing. Nothing else matters. Poetry is like that, too. It can create its own world. Emily knew how to live inside a poem. The older she got, the more poetry meant to her-- perhaps because it helped to recapture the all-consuming feelings that she experienced as a child.

Emily completed her formal schooling in 1848. Now 18, she began to educate herself. She acquired new books, made new friends in Amherst. She loved to write and to receive letters--particularly on special occasions and holidays. Here she mentions her excitement about Valentine's Day: "The last week has been a merry one in Amherst, & notes have flown around like, snowflakes." (Emily was creative not only with words, but with punctuation!)

Emily was very close to her brother and always took an interest in his schooling and his friends. Austin courted a local girl, Susan Gilbert, and Emily became her friend. When the two girls were apart, Emily wrote her "Susie" long letters telling her how much she missed her and reporting on events at home and on her state of mind. Here is a bulletin on her mood that Emily, then 21, sent to Susie: "I regret to inform you that at 3. o'clock yesterday, my mind came to a stand, and has since then been stationary."

The young Emily enjoyed nothing more than entertaining her friends and family with her letters,. Quite naturally, she elaborated on details taken from her own life, turning them into stories and inviting others to join in her play. Although apparently she was not writing poetry yet, her early letters begin to introduce what will become important themes in her work. She speculates on immortality and on the possibilities of an afterlife: "To live, and die, and mount again in triumphant body, and *next* time, try the upper air--is no schoolboy theme!" Emily is perhaps beginning to wonder how she might treat such a theme now that she is grown old enough actually to ponder it. She is caught between her enjoyment of the now and her curiosity about forever.

> *As for Emily, she was not withdrawn or exclusive, really. She was watching for the rewarding person to come, but she was a very busy person herself. She had to think--she was the only one of us who had to do that.*
>
> --Lavinia Dickinson,
> Emily's sister

A series of letters Emily wrote to Susan Gilbert in 1854 illustrates her increasing focus on life after death. Concerned about Edward Dickinson's dominance over his son, Susan had convinced Austin to move away from Amherst. When she and Austin went to Michigan, Emily responded with rage, equating their "betrayal" with death: "You need not fear to leave me lest I should be alone, for I often part with things . . . I have loved, --sometimes to the grave, and sometimes to an oblivion rather bitterer than death. . . ."

All was set right between the friends the next year when Austin and Susan returned to Amherst to stay. But the extreme emotion Emily's letters convey remained a part of her character. Her friend, Thomas Wentworth Higginson, once commented, "I never was with any one who drained my nerve power so much. Without touching me, she drew from me. I am glad not to live near her. She often thought me tired. . . ." And her dual focus on the sensations of the physical world and the shadowy nature of the afterlife helped shape Emily's growth as an artist.

Points to ponder

- What aspects of Emily Dickinson's life may have driven her to write poetry?

- What are Emily's thoughts about the differences between being an adult and a child? Why might her thoughts stimulate her to think about an afterlife?

- Is there a sense in which writing letters is a form of self-discipline?

CHAPTER 3
To Be Great--"Like Mr. Michael Angelo"

Although Emily had been composing short poems for years and including them in her correspondence--in fact, many of her letters read like poems--it was not until the late 1850s that she began to think of herself as a poet. Her letters from that period reveal that she was growing more and more interested in art. To be a great artist is to achieve a kind of immortality. You can live forever in other peoples' imaginations. She confessed to a friend that she wished to be great "like Mr. Michael Angelo," the Renaissance master of painting and sculpture. Also during this period, she began the habit of sewing together packets of her poems into little "booklets."

But Emily did not think of capturing the world's attention--at least not that of the here and now. She was content, she said, with friends, who made up her "estate," the sum of her wealth. For Emily, the letters and. later, poems, she sent her friends were gifts, treasures she wanted to share as proof of her loving devotion. In late December of 1858, Emily sent a poem to her sister-in-law, Susan Gilbert, in celebration of Susan's 28th birthday. Emily's poem imagines Susan as a bird who has built her nest in the Dickinson family tree and has thus "Builded our hearts among."

Letter writing and poetry composition began to blend into each other as Emily addressed more and more poems to her family and friends, using them as a kind of sounding board for her attempts at self-expression. Poetry became her constant companion. Like many 19th-century women, Emily engaged in needlework and other domestic pursuits, but she admitted that she often daydreamed while sewing, sometimes stopping altogether to "build a castle in the air."

Emily had a way of turning phrases to her advantage. While others might think her a recluse--someone who almost never went out into the world--she reversed this way of thinking about staying at home: "Father is in New York, and Vinnie [Emily's sister Lavinia] in Boston--while Mother and I for greater celebrity, are remaining at home." And in a curious way, Emily was proved right. It was her very reclusiveness--her creation of a vast poetic universe out of her own small domestic sphere--that would eventually bring her fame.

In fact, Emily made fun of people who thought they had to travel and to have adventures abroad to become famous. Life in public often provoked her scorn--as in these well known lines:

> How dreary to be somebody
> How public, like a frog
> To tell your name the livelong day
> To an admiring bog.

That last word of this poem, which conjures up the image of a swamp or marsh, suggests how distasteful public notice seemed to Emily. It would mean getting smeared with attention that would stick to her in unpleasant ways--bogging her down, so to speak.

Alice James, the sister of the novelist Henry James, appreciated Emily's aloofness. To Alice, Emily's poetry seemed more original because it was not infected with other peoples' ideas or with the desire to please the public. To Alice, Emily's work was the perfect expression of the aspiring soul.

Of course, why Emily turned to poetry remains something of a mystery. Certainly her New England background and the strong influence of religion played a part. In fact, it was largely because religion alone was not enough to satisfy her curiosity about existence that poetry became Emily's vehicle for exploring the complexities of life and death..

Emily's most productive years as a poet coincided with the Civil War (1861-1865), and of course thoughts about the deaths of soldiers were never very far from her mind during this period. In one letter, she mentions that "Mrs. Adams had news of the death of her boy to-day at Annapolis. . . . Another died in October--from fever caught in the camp."

As her mother grew increasingly frail and ill, Emily felt her duty was at home. More importantly, her home and "estate" of friends represented a kind of security that Emily sought in a world filled with human loss. It was much more common for women in the 19th century to die in childbirth, and for children to lose their brothers and sisters early to diseases that can be cured today. In general, people had shorter life spans than they do today, and Emily sat by many deathbeds in Amherst.

When Emily's Aunt Lavinia died, a distraught Emily wrote to her sister: "I sob and cry till I can hardly see my way 'round the house again. . . . And I thought she would live I wanted her to live so, I thought she could not die!"

Emily had to find a way to express her anxiety, and her poems portray many encounters with death. Compare her distress over her Aunt Lavinia's passing with the calm and steady language of the following lines:

> The eyes glaze once, and that is death.
> Impossible to feign
> The beads upon the forehead
> By homely anguish strung.

Here is death as an everyday worry, but also death that must be confronted honestly and directly. A dying person's eyes do lose focus, and there is no point in denying this evidence of the end of life. But acknowledging its presence is also a way for Emily to discipline and cope with her feelings. The beads of sweat are examples of "homely anguish," the everyday suffering that Emily shows she is familiar with. To be homely is to be plain, to be honest, and to not hide anything. Emily's poems seek to reveal such "homely" but important truths about how people should behave.

> *Such things could have come only from a woman's heart to which the experiences in a New England town have brought more knowledge of death than of life.*
>
> --William D. Howells,
> American critic and novelist

That death was often the subject of Emily's poems does not mean she was a sorrowful person. Her letters show her to be lively and funny. But she measured her happiness by the sorrow she knew was always waiting to strike. Her very awareness of death was part of her self-discipline: it made her stronger and better able to appreciate the joys of life as well as its unhappiness. And her poetry provided her with a release, a means of coping with life's ups and downs.

Points to ponder

- What did being great mean to Emily Dickinson?

- How did Emily's awareness of death contribute to her ideas of greatness and self-discipline?

- What is the difference between the way Emily confronts death in her letters and in her poems?

CHAPTER 4
Love and War and Fame

Although Emily thought long and hard about death, she did not take refuge in religion or console herself with the assurance of an afterlife. Living every day, she pointed out, was a challenge to religious belief. Human beings, by definition, are not divine, and therefore have trouble maintaining their faith. Or, as Emily put it more colorfully, "The Dust like the Mosquito, buzzes round my faith."

Emily wanted to believe in eternity, but she was also a very hardheaded, sensible adult. Think about these shrewd lines she enclosed in a letter to one of her male friends:

> "Faith" is a fine invention
> When Gentlemen can *see--*

> But *Microscopes* are prudent
> In an Emergency.

Emily Dickinson was a modern woman. She did not take things on faith when she knew there was knowledge to be had. But she also never made greater claims for human knowledge than could be justified.

The Civil War years were a trial for her and for her community. She did not deal with the war directly in her poetry, or even very much in her letters. Yet the sheer intensity of this national tragedy surely touched her and made her think even more deeply about the life-and-death issues that mark her greatest poetry.

In 1862, Emily wrote more poetry than ever before. She also made one of her few significant attempts to find a more public audience for her poetry. And she fell in love.

Love was the subject that dominated many of the letters Emily wrote that year, "A love so big it scares her, rushing among her small heart--pushing aside the blood and leaving her faint (all) and white in the gust's arm--[.]" Emily's peculiar punctuation--she does not end her sentence with the expected period--captures the sudden, overwhelming, and breathtaking nature of her emotions. She also writes in the third person, as though she is trying to distance herself, a little, from her driving passion.

Whom did Emily love? No biographer has been able to say for sure, although the likely candidate is the Reverend Charles Wadsworth. It may be that Emily never told him of her feelings, since there is a letter from him expressing concern about Emily's distress that does not indicate any awareness that he may be the cause of it. "I am distressed beyond measure at your note, received this morning, " he wrote. "I can only imagine the affliction which has befallen, or is now befalling you. . . . I beg you to write me, though it be but a word."

> *[Austin] said that at different times Emily had been devoted to several men. He even went so far as to maintain that she had been several times in love, in her own way. But he denied that because of her devotion to any one man she forsook all others.*
>
> --Millicent Todd Bingham,
> daughter of Emily's friend,
> Mabel Loomis Todd

Emily received no romantic acknowledgment from the man she loved, and she does not seem to have been willing to confess her love to him. Instead, she sought the next best thing: a man who could appreciate her poetry. In 1862 she wrote to Thomas Wentworth Higginson, after he published an essay in the national magazine, *The Atlantic Monthly*, urging unknown writers to seek an audience for their work. Higginson was a well-known literary figure, and Emily sought his opinion of her poetry, asking, "Are you too deeply occupied to say if my Verse is alive?"

Higginson did see life in Emily's poetry, although he also thought it could be improved. She reacted well to his criticism, but it was clear that she was not going to follow his advice. Higginson gave good advice for his time, but he did not fully realize that Emily Dickinson was writing not just for the popular tastes of mid-19th-century America, but also for the ages. She was not trying to write about feelings in words and phrases that everyone knew. She was trying to say new things using fresh words and in an original style.

Higginson was puzzled, for example, by all the dashes she put in her poems. He proposed using conventional punctuation marks such as commas and periods. He called her style "spasmodic," thinking perhaps of her tendency to jump swiftly from line to line and word to word. But Emily was imitating the way the mind jumps and the fact that thoughts often came in rapid succession. The experiences she described were abrupt, elusive, and mysterious. They could not be neatly tied up in ordinary, grammatically correct sentences.

She had few literary influences. For example, she never read the work of the greatest poet of the age, Walt Whitman. She preferred the work of some of her female contemporaries, such as the novelist George Eliot (the pen name for Mary Ann Evans) and the poet Elizabeth Barrett Browning, but their more conventional styles had little apparent impact on her writing

When Higginson asked Emily about her companions, she named not people but the hills, sundown, and a dog--implying how at one she felt with nature and how singular she felt in human company. What Higginson failed to appreciate was that Emily had a mind of her own and that her poetic style reflected an original sensibility and owed much to her relative lack of society. Certainly she wanted his approval. If she was suffering from disappointment in love, this male authority figure might have given her some comfort. Yet she imposed a discipline on herself that made it impossible for her simply to accept advice that was well meant but also ignorant of what she was trying to accomplish.

Fame, Emily knew, could be based simply on familiarity. A person becomes famous because she does things other people readily understand to be great. Emily, in contrast, sought recognition for precisely the opposite behavior: a quest for a unique form of expression. She would seek fame only on her terms. To accept anyone else's would turn her life into that bog that her poem so memorably disdains. In 1866, when Susan Dickinson published one of her sister-in-law's poems in a local newspaper without Emily's permission, the poet reacted with outrage, declaring, "it was robbed of me." The publication of "A narrow fellow in the grass" in *The Springfield Republican* marked one of the only times during her life that Emily's literary creations appeared in print.

Points to ponder

- How did Emily's falling in love influence her attitude toward her poetry?

- Even when she fell in love, Emily Dickinson does not seem to have abandoned the self-discipline that distinguished her as a person and as a poet. Why might she have remained so committed to her creative goals?

- What, in Emily's view, is the relationship between achievement and fame?

CHAPTER 5
The Aftermath

Emily continued her correspondence with Thomas Wentworth Higginson. She feared for his safety during the war when he became a colonel and led men into battle. Her own troubles and the nation's woes often mixed together in her mind. In 1861, she developed eye problems. The next year she began to fear she would go blind. In April of 1862, she wrote Higginson of "a terror--since September--I could tell to none--and so I sing, as the Boy does by the Burying Ground--because I am afraid." Emily did not say what caused this "terror," and later critics have attributed it to her difficulties in seeing, to disappointment in love, and to anxiety about the Civil War. In reality, the three could all have been connected for Emily. In 1864 and 1865, she was obliged to spend long periods in Cambridge, Massachusetts, undergoing medical treatments. During this period--at the same time the nation was suffering some of its darkest days--Emily was not permitted to read or write. It is little wonder that the poet experienced such a sense of desperation.

Yet an individual's fate and a country's were not the same and could not, in Emily's view, be understood in terms of one another. As she said to her friends, "Sorrow seems more general than it did, and not the estate of a few persons, since the war began; and if the anguish of others helped one with one's own, now would be many medicines."

After the war, Emily seems to have temporarily lost her energy for poetry. She also seems to have written fewer letters, although some of them have probably been lost. It would be natural, however, to experience a letdown after the intensity of the war years. An individual and a nation can suffer only so much. There has to be a lull, a phase when things seem dormant. As Emily so memorably wrote in one of her poems: "After great pain, a formal feeling comes."

Emily realized that she had been through a number of ordeals. She wrote to Thomas Wentworth Higginson, "You were not aware that you saved my Life." In many ways, this man was her outlet to the world, and his recognition was for her the equivalent of the world's acknowledgment of her gifts. Very few of her poems had been published, but the important thing was that she had made her contact with this important man.

Higginson was drawn to Dickinson almost in spite of himself. He still had trouble understanding her poetry, but he paid tribute to her powers as a writer. "Sometimes I take out your letters & verses, dear friend, and when I feel their strange power, it is not strange that I find it hard to write & that long months pass," he wrote in about the year 1869. He thought of her as surrounded by a "fiery mist," and he doubted he could ever penetrate to the heart of her passion. He was astounded by the profundity of her thoughts, wondering how someone who lived so much by herself could be so perceptive.

> *We shall never learn where she got the rich quality of her mind.*
>
> --Allen Tate,
> poet and literary critic

This was the very point about Emily Dickinson: She had pared down her life so as to give the world her full attention. She had adopted the discipline of the creative person who does not allow external events to distract her. Studying the world was, in fact, her discipline. Higginson wanted her to come to Boston and to take part in society there, but Emily evidently believed that such travel and society were contrary to the requirements of her genius. Events--her mother's illness, her spinster status, her eye problems--might have brought Emily to the decision never again to leave the Homestead, but the point is that she made a conscious decision to give up the world for her art. By the time the Civil War was over, Emily, too, seems to have reached the end of her own internal battle.

Points to ponder

- Why do you think Emily wrote fewer poems after the Civil War?

- Why do you suppose it was so hard for Colonel Higginson to understand Emily's quiet life and poetry?

- How do you think discipline applies to the creative process?

- What do you think Colonel Dickinson meant when he referred to Emily's "strange power"?

CHAPTER 6
Revival and Loss

In 1870, Emily Dickinson entered her fortieth year. In the spring, after she had three times refused his invitations to visit him and his family in Boston, Colonel Higginson finally came to Amherst. Emily appeared to him to be shy, even childlike. Writing to his wife about the meeting, Higginson commented, "[A]n instinct told me that the slightest attempt at direct cross-examination would make her withdraw into her shell; I could only sit still and watch, as one does in the woods. I must name my bird without a gun . . . ."

Higginson's comparison of Emily with a bird was quite right, for that is how she thought of herself and of the sense of life she was trying to capture in her writing, but he did not really understand her any more than he understood her poetry. She was careful about sharing her feelings. No one could penetrate her privacy or see more of her imaginative world than she was willing to reveal. And it probably is true that all those years of staying at home had made it difficult for her to talk to anyone other than her family and closest friends.

> *Austin smiles. He says Emily definitely posed in those letters [to Higginson], he knows her thoroughly, through and through, as no one else ever did.*
>
> --Mabel Loomis Todd, Emily's friend and Austin's lover

About this time, Emily began writing more letters, seeming to revive from the postwar slump that had dulled her creativity. A key to her mood is revealed in her exclamation, "I find ecstasy in living--the merest sense of living is joy enough." She also wrote some of her most beautiful poems in the early 1870s. But she was also worried during this period about her father's health. When he died on June 16, 1874, Emily's words reflected the same disciplined, calm attitude towards death and immortality found in her poetry. She wrote to close friends: "Father does not live with us now--he lives in a new house." She cried, though, for a parent who she described as "pure and terrible." Terrible, in her 19th-century vocabulary, suggested the solemn and careworn aspect of a man who felt so much responsibility towards his family and community. Emily missed him keenly, and as she indicated to Higginson, she felt she had lost the only real parent she ever had: "I always ran Home to Awe when a child, if anything befell me. He was an awful Mother, but I liked him better than none."

Edward Dickinson's death closed another phase in Emily's life. She would gradually withdraw even further from human company. Letters became even more precious to her, although she seems to have written fewer poems in the first years after her father's death. She would resume her creative life only gradually, still producing poems that remained of very high quality. Continuing to write poetry in the face of human loss was an act of courage. As one of her female friends suggested, Emily was daring.

> *Her verses all show a strange cadence of inner rhythmical music.*
>
> --Mabel Loomis Todd,
> one of Emily's friends

Emily herself referred to her life as "simple and stern." She had not lived so as to embarrass anyone, she pointed out. And she did not mind at all that she seemed a bit of a riddle to others. Many of her poems in fact take the form of riddles, such as one about a train that begins:

> I like to see it lap the Miles--
> And lick the Valleys up--
> And stop to feed itself at Tanks--
> And then--prodigious step

More often then not, though, her poetry involved a great deal of self-inspection. She had grown up in a New England town in the first half of the 19th century, and her Puritan heritage had taught her that the individual has a personal relationship with God. This habit of mind sometimes resulted in poems that are clearly religious. Sometimes, however, her thoughtfulness produced poems about her own ability to think about thinking, about how the world at first seems within our grasp, then we lose it. Ideas come and go, flitting through the mind, yet there is also the sense in her poetry that words can capture the thought process--and sometimes the precious thought itself.

Here is a poem of hers that speaks directly to this point. It reads as if Emily were right here addressing herself to you. She seems to be confiding an awareness of what it means to be a thinking human being. The poem itself, in other words, is about revival and loss, and how poetry can represent both:

> A Thought went up my mind today--
> That I have had before--
> But did not finish--some way back--
> I could not fix the Year--
>
> Nor where it went--nor why it came
> The second time to me--
> Nor definitely, what it was--
> Have I the Art to say--
>
> But somewhere--in my Soul--I know
> I've met the Thing before--
> It just reminded me--'twas all--
> And came my way no more—

Who has not experienced that feeling of knowing something, then losing that knowledge, then almost regaining it and wondering where it went, and why it comes no more? But only Emily Dickinson could have captured this experience in words and set them down on paper so creatively. She was writing at the top of her form.

Points to ponder

- Compare Higginson's and Todd's comments on Emily as person and poet. What is the connection between her personality and her poetry?

- Do you think Emily's poetry helped her to live?

- How would you describe the rhythm of Emily's poetry? Is that rhythm somehow connected to the way she lived her life?

CHAPTER 7
"Home is so far from Home"

By the mid 1870s, Emily Dickinson had withdrawn even further into herself and into her home life. Letters became one of her only avenues of communication with others. She delighted in writing about her observations of nature. Deaths of old friends continued to alarm her, but she sustained herself with friendships with Helen Hunt Jackson, one of the leading American poets of her time, and with Judge Otis Lord, with whom Emily appears to have fallen in love. Colonel Higginson had recommended Emily's poetry to Jackson, and Judge Lord had been a lifelong friend of Emily's father.

When Judge Lord's wife died in 1877, he and Emily drew closer. They may even have thought of marrying, judging by the affection expressed in their letters to one another. She called him "Sweet One," and she spoke of wanting to "lie so near your longing." She spoke openly of her love for him, which was like a "Fever with nearness to your blissful words." But writing about her passion proved easier than acting upon it. Evidently it was too late for Emily to make such a momentous change in her life. One of her letters appears to put off Lord's marriage proposal: "Don't you know you are happiest while I withhold and not confer--" In a similar mood, she wrote: "Don't you know that 'No' is the wildest word we consign to language?" As one Dickinson critic suggests, marrying Lord might have been extraordinarily disruptive to the daily discipline Emily had created for herself. Emily's relationship with Judge Lord gave rise to gossip. As some of her more sensual poems imply, she may have had more than one physical relationship with a man. In any event, her relationship with Judge Lord caused one Amherst resident to regard Emily as anything but a shy, retiring spinster. Emily was, "a little hussy. . . . Loose morals. She was crazy about men. Even tried to get Judge Lord. Insane, too," Abbie Farley, Judge Lord's niece and housekeeper, later remarked.

One of Emily's other suitors is said to have been Samuel Bowles, editor of the *Springfield Republican* and a longtime friend of the Dickinson family. He was a shrewd, energetic, and charismatic man who appealed greatly to women. Sometime around 1877, he is said to have come courting Emily. When she refused to come downstairs to meet him, he exclaimed: "Emily, you damned rascal! No more of this nonsense! I've traveled all the way from Springfield to see you. Come down at once." Perhaps she needed such goads in her life. For the story goes that she did come right down and was never more amusing.

> *[T]hese relationships combine to suggest a lethal conviction at the core of Dickinson's nature: deep affection for anyone outside the immediate family and passionate love both necessarily entail separation.*
>
> --Cynthia Griffin Wolff,
> Dickinson biographer

Bowles might well have said such things to Dickinson. Certainly her writer friend, Helen Hunt Jackson, did. She told Emily that she had lived too long out of the sunlight--meaning that Emily should emerge from her seclusion and take a more active part in the world. To Helen, the delicate Emily seemed but a wisp of a woman. She made Helen think of herself as a big, stupid ox. But Helen also sensed Emily's great strength as a writer and wrote to Emily taking back some of her criticisms. Certainly Emily did not think of herself as a delicate little flower. Writing to an ailing Mrs. Higginson, Emily remarked: "I wish you were strong like me."

Nobody's Perfect

Emily Dickinson prided herself on her manners and the consideration she showed her friends. But sometimes her high spirits or her pride made her seem rude to others. How greatly she offended other people is difficult to say. To one correspondent she admitted: "I am much ashamed. I misbehaved last night. I would like to sit in the dust." Emily feared that inconsiderateness would lose her friends, and she seems to have been always quick to make amends.

Emily's melancholy sometimes got the best of her, as she confided to Colonel Higginson: "Home is so far from Home, since my Father died." She liked to watch the birds frolicking on her father's grave. But love brought a saving grace to her sad thoughts: "There is nothing sweeter than Honor, but Love, which is its sacred price."

Emily took heart from the example of women authors such as Charlotte Brontë and George Eliot. She often referred to their novels in her letters. She apparently liked the fact that these women had an audience--even if she would do little to court one of her own. Of Eliot's masterpiece, Emily said: "What do I think of *Middlemarch*? What do I think of glory--?" The success of these writers undoubtedly justified Emily's ambitions. Like her, they confidently used the everyday experiences of women to create great literature. She was especially fond of the poet Elizabeth Barrett Browning, perhaps because, as one critic suggests, Barrett Browning was so skillful at using female experience and attributes to convey universal truths. These writers also opened new worlds that allowed others, in turn, to find for themselves. Eliot, Dickinson concluded, is the "Lane to the Indies Columbus was looking for."

Seeming to adhere to her sentiment that "Home is so far from Home," Emily was reaching a point in her life when she paused to consider where she had been and where she was headed. Had she accomplished what she set out to do? She confided to Colonel Higginson both her doubts about her achievement and her hope that what she had done might be as good--and certainly different--from what she had intended:

The things we thought that we should do
We other things have done
But those peculiar industries
Have never been begun

The Lands we thought that we should seek
When large enough to run
By Speculation ceded
To Speculation's Son--

The Heaven, in which we hoped to pause
When Discipline was done
Untenable to Logic
But possibly the one—

Emily Dickinson's lines can be difficult to understand, but they usually yield a distinct feeling about life. In this case, she speculates on the patterns in human lives that may surprise and yet somehow fulfill--in strange and unanticipated ways--the hopes we have for them. The heaven she writes may be the Christian one, but it can also be the heaven of our hopes, the fine place we strive for by leading disciplined lives. The lands we seek can be like those Columbus discovered. In other words, we can lead adventurous lives. But these lands might also be the dwelling place of the imagination--the kind of realm that Emily visited every day in her poems.

Points to ponder

- What do you think Emily meant when she said home was so far from home?

- Why did Emily choose to remain at home when she seems to have had the opportunity to leave it and to marry?

- Emily uses the word discipline in the poem she sent to Colonel Higginson. Why was this word so important to her?

CHAPTER 8
"The Mind Alone without Corporeal Friend"

The last five years of Emily Dickinson's life were filled with deaths of friends and family members, including those of her 8-year-old nephew, Gilbert, and her mother, with whom Emily had grown increasingly close during her long illness. Emily's poetry became fragmentary, though her letters continued to reveal her wit and deep thinking.

Gilbert's loss was a deep one; Emily had derived so much joy from watching his antics. She had once overheard Gilbert trying to evade his Aunt Lavinia's cross-examination about chasing the cat:

> "Weren't you chasing Pussy," said Vinnie to Gilbert?
> "No--she was chasing herself"--

"But was'nt she running pretty fast?"
"Well, some slow and some fast" said the beguiling Villain.

This was just the sort of childish, but subtle wordplay that most appealed to Emily.

As always, Emily took solace in nature, saying, "any gift but spring seems a counterfeit, but the birds are such sweet neighbors they rebuke us all." She often used scenes from nature to describe her insights and memories. Watching the birds, for example, she remembered an April day when they gathered by her kitchen door, cold and frightened by the snowstorms that had made for a hard spring. Her father then went to the barn in his slippers, carrying back grain for them--and hiding himself from their view lest he embarrass them, Emily thought. And Emily had studied botany and had extraordinary knowledge about growing things. She often surprised her male companions and acquaintances who thought of her as a recluse who lacked concrete knowledge about the world outside her front door.

How did that girl know that a boggy field wasn't good for corn?

--Samuel Bowles,
editor of *The Springfield Republican*

Emily derived much pleasure from a friendship with Mabel Loomis Todd, who arrived in Amherst in the autumn of 1881, accompanying her husband, a teacher of astronomy. Mabel, who eventually became Austin's lover, never actually saw Emily's face, but she would become a devoted and perceptive reader of Emily's poetry, editing and publishing it after Emily's death. Beginning to falter in her writing, Emily wrote Mabel: "The little sentences I began and never finished--the little wells I dug and never filled--."

In March 1884, Judge Lord died, and shortly afterwards Emily suffered a nervous breakdown. She still continued to write letters, however, and she was cheered by the publication in 1885 of a biography of George Eliot written by her husband, John Cross. Emily had been anticipating this event for more than three years, writing off and on about the biography to several friends. Now Eliot, who had died in 1880, was in a sense resurrected.

But this period of revival was short-lived, for Emily had to endure the added blow of Helen Hunt Jackson's unexpected death in August 1885. At about this time Emily herself began to fail, taking to her bed and suffering prolonged periods of confusion. She managed a few short messages to close friends, but her poetry (which had begun to fall off in volume in the 1870s) now ceased altogether. On May 15, 1888, Emily died of what was diagnosed as Bright's Disease, a kidney ailment. After her death, her sister Lavinia was amazed to discover hundreds of poems and fragments jammed into Emily's desk. Not even Vinnie had known how dedicated Emily had been to her art and how productive a poet she was.

In many ways, though, writing letters had always been Emily's first love. Some of her letters are written virtually as poems; others contain drafts of poems--as though Emily were letting her friends into her poetry workshop. A letter written in 1882 sums up what she felt about correspondence; it also reflects her sense that letters are themselves works of art, composed in solitude and conferring on the writer a kind of everlasting life. Her words also serve as a fitting epitaph for Emily herself, who so often speaks to us even as she is addressing her friends: "A Letter always seemed like Immortality, for is it not the Mind Alone, without Corporeal Friend?"

Points to ponder

- Why might letters have been easier for Emily to write than poems when her health and spirits began to fail?

- How is a letter like immortality, according to Emily?

SUMMING UP A LIFE

Emily Dickinson gave a good deal to her friends, to her family, and to the world in her letters and poems. Yet she was also elusive and held back a good deal of herself. She did not mind being a mystery. In fact, she wrote that "The Riddle we can guess/We speedily despise." One of Emily's most important friends and correspondents in the last five years of her life, Mabel Loomis Todd, never even saw her face!

Although Emily had deep and intense feelings, she believed that they had to be disciplined and channeled into her poetry. She may have feared their open expression in love and in marriage. Like one of her favored authors, George Eliot, she had a strong sense of morality and distrusted self-indulgence. Yet Emily had a romantic streak, as evidenced in her fondness for Charlotte Brontë, the author of *Jane Eyre*, the story of a very spirited woman who refused to compromise her individuality. Emily saw the virtue of both authors, although she certainly leaned in Eliot's direction.

Emily had an adventurous imagination, but it was rooted in home life and in domesticity. As Jay Leyda, one of her biographers, recounts, she asked that after her death she be "carried out the back door, around through the garden, through the opened barn from front to back, and then through the grassy fields to the family plot, always in sight of the house." She asked that the six Irishmen who tended the Dickinson grounds carry her coffin.

The point of Emily's devotion to her home and to her poetry seems to be that she found in both a way of knowing herself, of finding out what she did best, and establishing routines and disciplines that helped her to cope with the disappointments and devastations of life. Life was hard for an imaginative woman in nineteenth-century America. Although poets such as Helen Hunt Jackson did make popular successes of their work, they did not share Emily's profound grasp of nature and of human suffering. They have been largely forgotten as literary figures, while Emily Dickinson's stature as a poet has continued to grow.

Perhaps Emily Dickinson's greatness can be partly explained by her daily devotion to the word. Her letters, as well as her poems, always seem precise--even when she is writing a thank you note or some other minor message to the world. Whether she is trying to be amusing or serious--or both--her close attention to language is surely what has accounted for her enduring reputation as a poet. And her courageous, disciplined devotion to literature certainly merits the highest praise.

AFTERWORD TO PARENTS

What does Emily Dickinson's life teach your son or daughter about self-discipline? How did Emily's devotion to her daily tasks at home and to her poetry reflect an ordered, well-spent life? Without her ability to govern her emotions and her thoughts, she surely could not have written such great poetry.

Dickinson's life also raises questions about how much each individual needs to partake of the outside world. Few people can or perhaps should try to lead the life of a recluse, which is what Dickinson has often been called. But it might be helpful to point out to your child that while Dickinson might have led a quiet, stay-at-home life, she also took an avid interest in her friends and kept busy not only writing but taking care of her mother. Dickinson found a way to reconcile her devotion to her family and to her work. That can be a difficult reconciliation to achieve, but it is one worth thinking about and striving towards.

It might also be worth stressing that Dickinson recognized that other women's lives--even other writer's lives-- need not be so quiet. She approved of women authors such as George Eliot and Charlotte Brontë, both of whom were more involved with society than she was. And Dickinson read their biographies and tried to learn as much about them as possible. She believed, in other words, in what today we call role models.

Finally, you might discuss with your child the extent to which we can come to know the world through what we experience at home and through what becomes available to us when we leave home. Even Emily Dickinson traveled to major cities such as Boston and Philadelphia. She chose to remain very close to home and family, but she also recognized the right and the necessity for others to be more active and social. Lessons might be learned from her life even for those who choose greater engagement outside of home, neighborhood, and community. The key to Dickinson's life is that she recognized at an early age that enormous self-discipline would be required if she were to achieve her artistic goals. This restraint called on her not so much to ignore the world as to seek her inspiration within herself. Her achievement clearly brought her pleasure during her lifetime and, afterwards, a kind of immortality.

BIBLIOGRAPHY

Benfey, Christopher, ed. *Emily Dickinson: Lives of a Poet.* New York: George Braziller, 1986.

A short reliable biography and an excellent introduction to the poet for younger readers.

Gudrun, Grabher, ed. *The Emily Dickinson Handbook.* Amherst: University of Massachusetts Press, 2005.

Contains chapters on biography, historical context, manuscripts, letters, studies of Dickinson's poetry, the influence and reception of her work, and descriptions of forthcoming articles and books about the poet.

Habegger, Alfred. *My Wars are Laid Away in Books: The Life of Emily Dickinson.* New York: Random House, 2001.

Recommended for mature readers, this biography makes use of recent feminist scholarship.

Johnson, Thomas H., ed. *The Letters of Emily Dickinson.* 3 vols. Cambridge, MA: Harvard University Press, 1960.

An invaluable, meticulously edited and annotated text.

_____. *The Poems of Emily Dickinson.* 3 vols. Cambridge, MA: Harvard University Press, 1955.

Johnson was the first scholar to re-establish a complete edition of Dickinson's poetry using her original punctuation.

Longsworth, Polly. *The World of Emily Dickinson.* New York: W. W. Norton, 1997.

Includes photographs, drawings, maps and other illustrations that help to visualize the world in which Dickinson wrote her poetry.

Martin, Wendy. *The Cambridge Introduction to Emily Dickinson.* Cambridge: Cambridge University Press, 2007.

Deals with the central issues in the poet's life and work as well as explaining the critical reception of her work. Consult this book to learn how Emily Dickinson became a major poet through the efforts of many scholars and critics.

Sewall, Richard B. *The Life of Emily Dickinson.* New York: Farrar, Straus & Giroux, 1974.

Still regarded as the standard biography of the poet.

Wineapple, Brenda. *White Heat: The Friendship of Emily Dickinson and Thomas Wentworth Higginson.* New York: Alfred A. Knopf, 2008.

> A revisionist work, in which Wineapple presents a much more sympathetic view of Higginson than is to be found in most accounts of his relationship with the poet.

Wolff, Cynthia Griffin. *Emily Dickinson.* New York: Alfred A. Knopf, 1986.

> Recommended only for advanced students of the poet's life and work.

GLOSSARY

Barrister. A lawyer who tries cases in court.

Bog. An area of wet, swampy ground.

Bright's Disease. Also known as nephritis, a chronic--sometimes fatal--inflammation of the kidneys.

Bur. The rough, prickly outer coating of some seeds.

Charismatic. Special quality that gives an individual the power to charm, influence, or inspire others.

Fugitive. A word used to describe fleeting or passing moments or feelings.

Hussy. A bold, mischievous, or immoral woman.

Melancholy. A gloomy, depressed state of mind.

Nervous Breakdown. A non-technical term used to describe a severe emotional disorder that usually leaves the sufferer incapable of leading a normal life for some time. *Burn out?*

Patron. An individual who supports, financially and emotionally, the creative work of a particular artist, group, or type of artistic endeavor.

Recluse. One who withdraws from the world into a solitary life.

Spasmodic. A word used to describe sudden outbursts of emotion or energy, it was used to describe a group of nineteenth-century English poets known for their extravagant use of language and excessive emotionalism.

Spinster. A woman who remains unmarried beyond the usual age for marriage.

www.ingramcontent.com/pod-product-compliance
Ingram Content Group UK Ltd.
Pitfield, Milton Keynes, MK11 3LW, UK
UKHW040948070425
5349UKWH00040B/301